P9-DEV-512

Whooping Cranes

Precious McKenzie

EYE to EYE
with Endangered Species

ROURKE PUBLISHING
Vero Beach, Florida 32964

© 2010 Rourke Publishing LLC

www.rourkepublishing.com

PHOTO CREDITS: Title page, 4, 5: © Allan Mueller; 2, 3: © McKevin Shaughnessy; 6, 7, 8, 9, 23, 24 : © Robert Blanchard; 8, 9: © Samir Arora; 10, 11: © B.G. Smith ; 12: © International Crane Foundation, Baraboo, Wisconsin; 12, 13, 23: © Ian McDonnell; 13: © International Crane Foundation, Baraboo, Wisconsin.; 14, 15: © Terry Healy; 15: © Marcia Straub; 16: © Andrew Gentry, © Wojtek Kryczka, © Jameson Weston; 16, 17: © © Eduardo Leite; 17: © Nick M. Do, © Lev Ezhov, © Dirk Rietschel, © Rainer Junker, © Tomasz Zachariasz; 18, 19: © Andrea Gingerich; 19: © jan kranendonk; 20, 21: © TK Edens; 20: © westphalia; 21: © AP Images; 22: © Peter Blottman

Editor: Jeanne Sturm
Cover design by Teri Intzegian
Page design by Heather Botto

Library of Congress Cataloging-in-Publication Data

McKenzie, Precious.
 Whooping cranes / Precious McKenzie.
   p. cm. -- (Eye to eye with endangered species)
 Includes index.
 ISBN 978-1-60694-401-1 (hard cover)
 ISBN 978-1-60694-840-8 (soft cover)
 1. Whooping crane--Juvenile literature. I. Title.
 QL696.G84M377 2010
 598.3'2--dc22
                                    2009005992

Printed in the USA

CG/CG

ROURKE PUBLISHING

www.rourkepublishing.com - rourke@rourkepublishing.com
Post Office Box 643328 Vero Beach, Florida 32964

Table of Contents

Whooping Cranes

What's the tallest bird in North America? If you guessed the whooping crane, then you are correct! The whooping crane is also one of the most studied birds in North America. Many scientists in the United States and Canada are concerned about this **endangered** species.

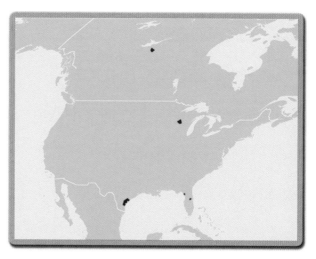

Whooping Crane Habitat Regions

Fifty years ago, whooping cranes were almost extinct. Today, they are making a comeback.

A Close Call for the Crane Population

In the past, whooping cranes were found in large numbers in North America. However, human and animal predators have not helped the whooping crane population. By the 1950s there were only sixteen whooping cranes left! Today, thanks to **conservationists**, there are approximately four hundred whooping cranes in the wild.

Whooping cranes prefer marshland and estuaries. Here they are able to find delicious food such as clams and frogs.

Fun Fact

Scientists use radio transmitters attached to the cranes in order to track their migratory patterns. They use this data to study the birds' lifestyle.

A Stately Bird

Whooping cranes are tall, majestic birds. They stand almost 5 feet (1.5 meters) tall. They have white feathers on their bodies, with black wingtips. Whooping cranes have red foreheads and cheeks. Their legs are long and gray, and their beaks are long and pointed. When in flight, the whooping crane's **wingspan** is almost 10 feet (3 meters) across.

We know this is an adult crane because it is white and has a red head. A juvenile whooping crane is cinnamon colored and does not have red on its head.

Life at the Water's Edge

Whooping cranes love to be near water. They spend their lives near rivers, freshwater **marshes**, lakes, and estuaries. Whooping cranes build their nests near water. They also dine on small creatures that live there.

Whooping cranes prefer to eat snails, frogs, leeches, and small fish. A crane will push its long beak around in the water, overturning rocks, searching for tasty snacks.

Whooping Crane Families

Male and female whooping cranes mate for life. The female crane lays two eggs in a large nest built on the ground. Most of the time, only one chick survives. The adult male and female cranes raise their chick. They take turns guarding the territory surrounding the nest.

When the young crane is 11 months old it no longer requires its parents' care. It is all grown up!

Scientists consider whooping cranes to be excellent parents. These birds are watchful and careful with their chicks.

Crane Communication

Because of their unique vocalizations, whooping cranes are affectionately known as whoopers. Their calls sound like loud rattling noises. Often, when cranes call, they dance. Whoopers stand upright and then dip, jump, and flap their wings.

Mated pairs of cranes call out as one. The female's call is higher pitched and the male's is lower. Each time the female makes her two shorter calls, the male joins in with one long call.

Juvenile whooping cranes practice body language. Each dip, jump, and turn means something important for cranes. This is all part of the crane communication process.

Crane Cravings

Cranes are omnivores, which means they eat meat and plants. Their favorite meats include **crustaceans**, **mollusks**, frogs, snakes, and insects. They also eat grains and acorns.

Grains

Acorns

Crustacean

Frog

Snake

Mollusk

Insect

Bears, bobcats, and raccoons are threats to whooping cranes because these animals dine on whooping crane eggs. Humans pose a larger threat to the cranes. Through farming and urbanization, people destroy the whooping crane's natural habitat.

Fun Fact

*Conservationists joined forces and created whooping crane **preservation** areas. One flock of whooping cranes summers in the Necedah National Wildlife Refuge in Wisconsin. Then, in the winter, these whoopers **migrate** south to the Chassahowitzka National Wildlife Refuge in Florida.*

Whooping cranes need protected marshlands in order to survive. Congestion from cities, power lines, and pollution are threats to their survival.

Whoopers and Ultralight Aircraft

To help reestablish the whooping crane population, biologists carefully monitor the cranes in **captivity**. Because the chicks are raised in captivity, the biologists must teach them how to migrate. The scientists teach the chicks to recognize the sound of an ultralight aircraft. Then they teach the young cranes how to run behind the aircraft. Eventually, the young cranes will follow the ultralight on their migration south.

Fun Fact

In Wisconsin, biologists dress up like adult cranes and raise whooping crane chicks.

Ultralight aircraft pilots, like Brooke Pennypacker pictured here, play an important role in saving whooping cranes. Without these brave pilots, young whooping cranes would have a very difficult time finding protected marshlands.

How You Can Help

We must not allow North America's largest bird to disappear. You can help save the whooper from **extinction**. Write letters to your state representatives asking them to sign **legislation** that protects the whooping cranes' wetland habitats.

You can also volunteer to clean up local wetlands and parks. This will help keep the Earth clean for all species of birds and animals, including the whooping crane.

Tracking the rare whooping crane is not easy. So, if you live near a whooping crane habitat and you spot wild whooping cranes, report it to the United States Fish and Wildlife Service. Be sure to tell them where and when you saw the cranes and how many you saw. Your field work will help scientists track and protect these magnificent birds.

Glossary

captivity (kap-TIV-uh-tee): living under the control of humans

conservationists (kon-sur-VAY-shuhn-ists): people who protect natural resources

crustaceans (kruhss-TAY-shuhnz): animals with hard shells that live in the water, such as crabs, crayfish, shrimp, and lobsters

endangered (en-DAYN-jurd): threatened with extinction

extinction (ek-STINGKT-shuhn): when an animal species dies out

legislation (lej-uh-SLAY-shuhn): a law made by members of government

marshes (MARSH-ez): low-lying areas with water and tall grasses

migrate (MYE-grate): to travel from one climate to another

mollusks (MOL-uhsks): soft-bodied animals, such as clams and snails, that have a shell and live in the ocean

preservation (prez-ur-VA-shuhn): protection from damage

wingspan (WING-span): distance from the tip of one wing to the tip of the other

Index

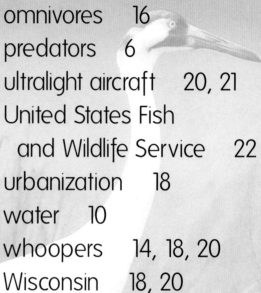

Websites to Visit

animals.nationalgeographic.com/animals/birds/whooping-crane.html

www.dnr.state.wi.us/Org/caer/ce/eek/critter/bird/crane.htm

www.learner.org/jnorth/tm/crane/jr/WildCapCompAns3.html

About the Author

Precious McKenzie has loved animals and reading all of her life. She was born in Ohio but has spent most of her life in south Florida, traipsing through the Everglades. Her love of children and literature led her to earn degrees in education and English from the University of South Florida. She currently lives in Florida with her husband and three children.